STUDENTS IN DANGER:

Survivors of School Violence

STUDENTS IN DANGER:

Survivors of School Violence

Rae Simons

 Mason Crest Publishers

STUDENTS IN DANGER: Survivors of School Violence

MASON CREST PUBLISHERS INC.
370 Reed Road
Broomall, Pennsylvania 19008
(866)MCP-BOOK (toll free)
www.masoncrest.com

Because the stories in this series are told by real people, in some cases names have been changed to protect the privacy of the individuals.

First Printing
9 8 7 6 5 4 3 2 1

ISBN 978-1-4222-0449-8 (series)
ISBN 978-1-4222-1462-6 (series) (pbk.)

Library of Congress Cataloging-in-Publication Data

Simons, Rae, 1957–
  Students in danger : survivors of school violence / Rae Simons.
       p. cm. — (Survivors: ordinary people, extraordinary circumstances)
  Includes bibliographical references and index.
  ISBN 978-1-4222-0455-9 (hardback : alk. paper) — ISBN 978-1-4222-1468-8 (pbk. : alk. paper)
  1. School violence—United States. 2. School shootings—United States. 3. Schools—United States--Safety measures. I. Title.
  LB3013.32.S55 2009
  371.7'820973—dc22
                                        2008050333
Design by MK Bassett-Harvey.
Produced by Harding House Publishing Service, Inc.
www.hardinghousepages.com
Cover design by Andrew Mezvinsky.
Printed in The Hashimite Kingdom of Jordan.

CONTENTS

Introduction

Each of us is confronted with challenges and hardships in our daily lives. Some of us, however, have faced extraordinary challenges and severe adversity. Those who have lived—and often thrived—through affliction, illness, pain, tragedy, cruelty, fear, and even near-death experiences are known as survivors. We have much to learn from survivors and much to admire.

Survivors fascinate us. Notice how many books, movies, and television shows focus on individuals facing—and overcoming—extreme situations. *Robinson Crusoe* is probably the earliest example of this, followed by books like the *Swiss Family Robinson*. Even the old comedy *Gilligan's Island* appealed to this fascination, and today we have everything from the Tom Hanks' movie *Castaway* to the hit reality show *Survivor* and the popular TV show *Lost*.

What is it about survivors that appeals so much to us? Perhaps it's the message of hope they give us. These people have endured extreme challenges—and they've overcome them. They're ordinary people who faced extraordinary situations. And if they can do it, just maybe we can too.

This message is an appropriate one for young adults. After all, adolescence is a time of daily challenges. Change is everywhere in their lives, demanding that they adapt and cope with a constantly shifting reality. Their bodies change in response to increasing levels of sex hormones; their thinking processes change as their brains develop, allowing them to think in more abstract ways; their social lives change as new people and peers become more important. Suddenly, they experience the burning need to form their own identities. At the same time, their emotions are labile and unpredictable. The people they were as children may seem to have disappeared beneath the onslaught of new emotions, thoughts, and sensations. Young adults have to deal with every single one of these changes, all at the same time. Like many of the survivors whose stories are told in this series, adolescents' reality is often a frightening, confusing, and unfamiliar place.

Young adults are in crises that are no less real simply because these are crises we all live through (and most of us survive!) Like all survivors, young adults emerge from their crises transformed; they are not the people they were before. Many of them bear scars they will carry with them for life—and yet these scars can be integrated into their new identities. Scars may even become sources of strength.

In this book series, young adults will have opportunities to learn from individuals faced with tremendous struggles. Each individual has her own story, her own set of circumstances and challenges, and her own way of coping and surviving. Whether facing cancer or abuse, terrorism or natural disaster, genocide or school violence, all the survivors who tell their stories in this series have found the ability and will to carry on despite the trauma. They cope, persevere, persist, and live on as a person changed forever by the ordeal and suffering they endured. They offer hope and wisdom to young adults: if these people can do it, so can they!

These books offer a broad perspective on life and its challenges. They will allow young readers to become more self-aware of the demanding and difficult situations in their own lives—while at the same time becoming more compassionate toward those who have gone through the unthinkable traumas that occur in our world.

— Andrew M. Kleiman, M.D.

Chapter One

ARE OUR SCHOOLS SAFE? SURVIVING SCHOOL

The place was Red Lake, Minnesota, a small community near the Canadian border. The date was March 21, 2005. A sixteen-year-old killed his grandfather and girlfriend, and then, armed with several guns, went to the Red Lake High School. There, he passed through the metal detector, shot the unarmed school resource officer, and went on a ten-minute shooting rampage in the halls of the school. When he ended it by shooting himself, he had killed an English teacher and five students and had left seven wounded. In the investigation that followed, police learned that other students were involved in planning the attack, and a number of other students knew something was going to happen.

Violence in the Country

For years, the common conception was that violence only happened in inner-city schools. People believed that suburban and rural schools were safe from such happenings. These perceptions have changed. Taber, Alberta, is a small farming community. Red Lake, Minnesota, is a small town on an Ojibwa (Chippewa) reservation. Columbine is an upscale suburban community. The violence that occurred in these communities is not the same as that associated with inner-city gangs and drug culture. It is a different phenomenon, caused by other tensions than economic ones.

Several years earlier, a rash of school shootings occurred in places such as Moses Lake, Washington; Bethel, Alaska; Pearl, Mississippi; West Paducah, Kentucky; Jonesboro, Arkansas; Springfield, Oregon; and Columbine High School in Littleton, Colorado. And the problem wasn't confined to schools in the United States. There were also fatal episodes in schools in Scotland, Yemen, the Netherlands, Germany, and Sweden. Canadian schools had not had a fatal school shooting in

Canadian School Violence

Polls show that violence is of increasing concern in Canadian schools. A recent study revealed that violence is the top educational concern in Canada. Surveys indicate that teachers feel less safe at work. While shootings get the attention of the news media, other types of violent behaviors have also increased. These include everything from verbal abuse, to physical assaults and bullying. Canadian educators are taking the issue seriously.

twenty years, but on April 18, 1999, just eight days after the Columbine incident, a youth entered a high school in Taber, Alberta, and killed one student and seriously wounded another.

The horrifying news stories of senseless shootings in schools have given the impression that schools are a dangerous place to be, but national surveys have consistently found that school violence has not increased. Instead, a report issued in 2004 indicated

Though stories of school shootings may make school feel dangerous, students should not feel as though they have to be constantly afraid; school violence has not actually increased in recent years.

Youth and Violence

Homicide is the second-leading cause of death for persons ages fifteen to twenty-four. For African American youth, it is the leading cause of death. However, little of the violence reported for children and youth occurs in schools. Research has shown that students between the ages of five and nineteen were seventy times more likely to be murdered somewhere other than school.

that violent crime against students actually fell by 50 percent in the previous ten years. However, the perception of not being safe in schools remains. Even one school shooting is too much! Students in today's schools don't always feel safe.

WHAT MAKES SCHOOLS UNSAFE?

Where does the violence come from in schools? What are the roots that feed it? Without knowing the answers to those questions, it's difficult for school districts, for parents, and for students to know how to launch a defense against violence.

In the name of school safety, some schools require that students carry see-through backpacks; other schools have banned backpacks altogether. Some schools regularly search students' lockers for guns, knives, and other weapons.

But these measures seem to address the symptoms rather than the disease. It's like taking an aspirin for cancer. The pain may be masked, but the disease is still growing and festering.

What Is a Stereotype?

A stereotype is a fixed, commonly-held notion or image of a person or group that's based on an oversimplification of some observed or imagined trait. Stereotypes assume that whatever is believed about a group is typical for each individual within that group.

Most stereotypes tend to make us feel superior in some way to the person or group being stereotyped. Not all stereotypes are negative, however; some are positive—"black men are good at basketball" or "Asian students are smart"—but that doesn't make them true. They ignore individuals' uniqueness. They make assumptions that may or may not be accurate.

The average high school has its share of stereotypes—lumping a certain kind of person together, ignoring all the ways that each person is unique. These stereotypes are often expressed with a single word or phrase: "jock," "nerd," "goth," "prep," or "geek." The images these words call to mind are easily recognized and understood by others who share the same views. Stereotypes become dangerous when we continue to hold onto our mental images despite new evidence, when we refuse to even see that there *is* new evidence. That's when they turn into prejudice.

WHO IS IT THAT MAKES SCHOOLS VIOLENT?

"He was a quiet kid. Who would have thought he would do something like that."

"They dressed different from the other kids. They were outsiders."

"He was weird."

"I didn't really know him. He was really studious and he never said much."

"He seemed nice. But he didn't really hang out with anyone."

These are the typical comments from the classmates of people who committed violence in schools.

The common element of all these comments? The kids involved felt like they were outsiders. They were isolated from the rest of the students. Often, they were the nerds, the geeks, the goths; they belonged to a stereotype that set them apart.

Many of these students were the victims of small acts of violence themselves. Maybe no one pointed a gun at them—but they did get shoved around in the locker room after gym class. Or the violence may have been verbal only, taunts and insults that made them feel inferior. In other words, these kids were bullied.

People who feel left out or isolated from others, perhaps because of teasing or bullying, may be more likely to commit acts of violence.

BULLYING AND SCHOOL VIOLENCE

According to the U.S. National Mental Health Information Center, bullying is:

> when one or more persons repeatedly say or do hurtful things to another person who has problems defending himself or herself. Direct bullying usually involves hitting, kicking, or making

President George W. Bush, seen here shaking hands with former Columbine student Craig Scott, attended a panel on School Safety. At the panel, held on October 10, 2006, President Bush said "Our parents I know want to be able to send their child or children to schools that are safe places."

DRUG FREE

GUN FREE
SCHOOL ZONE
VIOLATORS WILL FACE SEVERE
FEDERAL STATE AND LOCAL
CRIMINAL PENALTIES

insults, offensive and sneering comments, or threats. Repeatedly teasing someone who clearly shows signs of distress is also recognized as bullying. However, indirect bullying—the experience of being excluded from a group of friends, being spoken ill of and being prevented from making friends—can be just as painful.

Drug Free, Gun Free school zones like the one pictured allow more strict punishments for those who break laws near school zones.

According to research done by America's Secret Service and the U.S. Department of Education involving 37 school shootings, including Columbine, about two-thirds of student shooters were bullied. Of course, most school bullying cases do not lead to school shootings—but sometimes they do. And like we said earlier, even one school shooting is too many!

Surviving middle school and high school is a challenge for many kids. They may not fear for their lives, but they do fear for their safety. Their self-esteem takes blow after blow, leaving wounds that can last a lifetime. Sometimes these are the kids who eventually explode and turn to violence themselves. Other times, their wounds merely fester inside them, kind of like the cancer we mentioned earlier.

Ultimately, it's often those who are innocent who get caught in the crossfire between bully and victim. In that case, survival takes on a whole new meaning. Now survival is literal, a matter of life and death.

But after the last gunshot has been fired, when all that's left are the news stories on television, how do these survivors continue to live? What does survival really mean to those who have lived through school violence?

A Serious Problem

The National Institutes of Health (2000) recently reported that in the United States alone, bullying affects more than 5 million students in grades 6 through 11. One out of 7 students reported being victimized Approximately 20 percent reported that they had bullied other students with the same frequency.

.   Major studies in Norway in the 1980s and 1990s with more than 150,000 students found that about 15 percent of students in primary and lower secondary school, or approximately one in seven students, were involved in bullying with a degree of regularity—as a victim, as a bully, or both. At least 5 percent (more than 1 in 20) of all students were involved in more serious bullying at least once a week.

Chapter Two

THE COLUMBINE SHOOTINGS: REACHING PAST OUR BOUNDARIES

On April 20, 1999, at Columbine High School near Denver, Colorado, two students pulled out guns and began shooting. When they were done, fifteen students were dead, including the shooters themselves, as well as a teacher. Twenty-three others were wounded.

Afterward, the nation reeled in shock and sorrow. This was the deadliest public school shooting that had ever happened in America. Governments, citizens, and school districts reexamined their laws and regulations. People tried to make sense of something that seemed too horrible to be possible. The struggle to put their worlds back together was even harder for Columbine's survivors, the students who had lived through the ordeal.

A SURVIVOR'S STORY

This is the HOPE Columbine Library which was built to replace the library where much of the shooting at the school took place.

When Marjorie Lindholm woke up on the morning of the Columbine shootings, she was thinking about a boy. She wasn't expecting anything out of the ordinary from the day, nothing more exciting than having a chance to talk to him. Marjorie was a sophomore who had just made the cheerleading squad; she was hoping to go on to become a doctor when she was older. Her plans for the future were made, her life on course. She certainly wasn't expecting that later that afternoon,

The HOPE Library was opened officially in 2001, a little more than two years after the shooting. The library is built using elements of the previous library, and paid for by donations from all over the country.

two students at her school would kill thirteen people. And she had no way of knowing how that would change her own life as well.

As Marjorie sat in her fifth-period class, taking a biology test, she heard something that sounded like rocks against a window. Her teacher told the class it was probably some sort of senior prank. "But, then," Marjorie told a reporter, "we heard screaming so horrible you'd never want to hear it again."

For the next four hours, Marjorie crouched in the classroom, listening to the turmoil in the rest of the building. Fire alarms blared. Her favorite teacher, Coach Sanders, died in the same room with her after being shot twice. "Dead bodies don't look like they do in the movies," Marjorie realized.

She told a reporter from WebMD, "I think with Columbine, people don't really realize, [the degree of emotional trauma depends

traumatized: having suffered an emotional or physical injury, often causing lasting damage.

on] kind of where you were at the school. If somebody was at the far end of it and ran out of the school right away, I don't think they were as **traumatized** as someone who was stuck in the library or the science room or saw someone shot. So I think there were lots of different levels of trauma that occurred with Columbine."

For months after the violence, Marjorie suffered with stomachaches and nightmares. She got sick with fevers again and again. Eventually, a month into her senior year, she dropped out of school. Sitting in a classroom

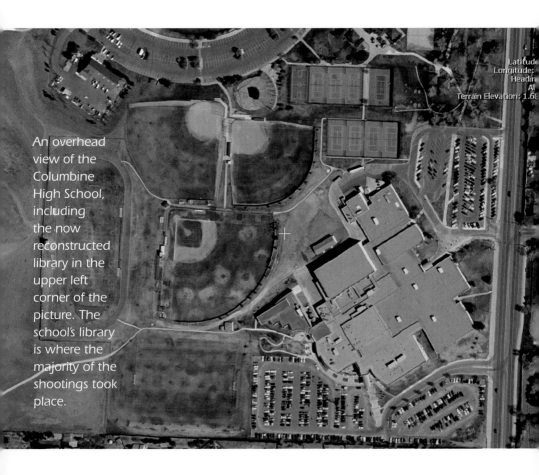

An overhead view of the Columbine High School, including the now reconstructed library in the upper left corner of the picture. The school's library is where the majority of the shootings took place.

Latitude
Longitude;
Headin
Al
Terrain Elevation: 1.6§

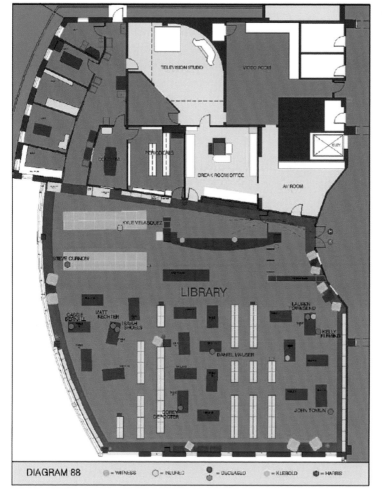

A map of the old library on the Columbine High School campus, which was rebuilt as the HOPE library two years later.

was something she could no longer handle. She earned her GED, but then she faced the same difficulties when she tried to attend college: classrooms had become places of terror for her. Her life had veered off track in a way she could never have anticipated—and she had no idea how to get it back on course.

"I didn't even deal with it for years," Marjorie told a reporter. "It just wasn't spoken about."

Not Just a Modern Phenomenon

People often assume that school violence is a product of our modern world. But the deadliest incidence of school violence actually took place more than 80 years ago.

The Bath School disaster is the name given to three bombings in Bath Township, Michigan, on May 18, 1927, an event that killed forty-five people and injured fifty-eight, most of them children in the second to sixth grades. The bomber was a school board member, Andrew Kehoe, who was upset by a property tax that had been levied to fund the construction of the school building. He blamed the additional tax for his own financial hardships. He had been secretly planting explosives in the school building for many months.

Her mother, a professional counselor, suggested that Marjorie start keeping a journal to help her confront her emotions and thoughts. That journal turned into a book: *A Columbine Survivor's Story.*

You might say that the violence in Columbine High School destroyed many lives, including Marjorie's, in addition to the fifteen people who actually died. But despite her struggles, Marjorie believes she has come out of this a better person and strives to make the most of her life. She switched to an online course of college study, and she tries to move ahead with her life, even though it's a different life than the one she'd once planned.

Marjorie hopes her book will help young people deal with their own traumas or hardships. "(The shootings) put in perspective the things I really care about," she said. "I feel more prepared for things now. Nothing can be worse than what I've faced."

Every time another school shooting happens, Marjorie reaches out to the survivors. She told WebMD,

> Usually, every time a school shooting happens, I try and contact at least one major news source and give out my email address so that the victims or anyone who needs to talk with me or anyone who's lived through it can contact me. . . . It's upsetting because it brings up my own issues, but in another way it doesn't feel like you're alone anymore. Not that I want anyone else to go through it. If they already have, it's kind of like, now it's us. We're a group. And we can get through it together. Some days I have hard days and I need help from other people. . . . I lean on them some days and they lean on me, and I think that's what you have to do. If you isolate yourself, then I think it leads to depression and anger and eventually a very unhealthy lifestyle.

THE OUTSIDERS' HEROES

After Columbine, people were scared . . . angry . . . sad. Some people hated the shooters. Others felt that that the shooters were victims as much as the others who died that day. And still others admired Eric Harris and

Factors That May Have Contributed to the Shooters' Actions

In the months after Columbine, many experts searched for the reasons behind Eric and Dylan's violence. They put forward several possible factors:

- high school cliques that excluded Eric and Dylan
- a climate of bullying that the Columbine school allowed
- the influence of violent video games
- the influence of heavy-metal lyrics

Ultimately, however, these are only theories. Eric and Dylan committed suicide after the shootings, so no one can ask them their reasons.

Dylan Klebold, the two young men responsible for the violence at Columbine.

For some young people, Eric and Dylan were symbols with whom they could identify. They were outsiders, kids who had had enough of being ignored, harassed, and bullied. They'd finally gotten angry and taken action.

This reaction scares people like Marjorie. She told WebMD:

I think that the way that the way media portrayed Columbine right when it happened kind of set Eric and Dylan as

The Faces of Evil?

According to psychologist David Danbury, human beings tend to cope with threats by "demonizing the danger." In other words, a person or thing that has caused death and destruction is seen as "absolute evil." This removes the need to try to understand what happened and instead allows people to respond with singleminded hatred in order to defend the community against danger. Danbury suggests that while this may have been a useful evolutionary technique in a more primitive world, it is not so useful in today's world. Instead, it tends to perpetuate a cycle of violence and danger that might otherwise be broken.

Granted that you can't tell a book by it's cover—but when you look at the faces of Eric and Dylan, the Columbine shooters, do they look like "absolute evil"?

these **icons** to so many people who were bullied and abused and with mental illness. And unfortunately that hasn't gone away. I think a lot of people want to do copycat shootings, and I think a lot of people want to prove a point by showing that they can also do it. And unfortunately, out of a school of thousands of people, it only takes one person . . . to do this to everyone. So even those few people [the outsiders who strike out]—

icons: symbols that represent a culture, idea, or event to a great number of people.

and they are just a few people—can just devastate millions of people because as you see, it affects the nation.

The ability to shake a nation is tremendous power for a young person who has felt ignored and insignificant for most of his life. Eric and Dylan may be dead—but in some kids' minds, they went out in a blaze of glory. The media's obsession with school violence feeds into this.

So what can we do to protect ourselves from a violence that springs to life out of loneliness and rejection? Marjorie recommends that people fight back against the imaginary boundaries that separate us.

I know there [are] cliques and there always will be, but if [people] could just be accepting for right now and make sure nobody's alone, even the weird kid that sits in the corner. You know, you have to watch out for everyone right now.

LEARNING FROM TRAGEDY

In North American culture, many people have the expectation that life *ought to be* safe and healthy and happy. Anything else is an affront to the "American way." We've been blessed with so much in this country; while other areas of the world deal with disease and war and famine, realities where death is an everyday occurrence, most of us in the

The memorial built at Columbine to honor the memory of the students killed, opened on September 21, 2007.

United States and Canada assume that we are **exempt** from these dangers.

When our vision of reality is shattered by something like what happened at Columbine—an outburst of deadly violence in an ordinary town on an ordinary day—we want to do whatever we can to make sure it never happens again. We want things to go back to "normal."

But Marjorie reminds us that "normal" may no longer be possible.

exempt: free from an obligation or duty.

Because this is a life-changing thing . . . when I walked into Columbine that day and when I walked out, I was a different person. . . . Everyone wants to act like it didn't happen. Everyone wants what they woke up with that morning—the normal family life. But unfortunately, once something like that happens, I don't know how realistic that is.

Incidents of school violence ask us to change ourselves. We need to examine who we are. Do we categorize people, set up boundary lines that include some people while they shut others out? Is there something inside us, in the way we and our friends act, or in the things we allow to go on around us that could contribute to a Columbine in our community?

LIFE GOES ON

After a tragedy—whether it's a school shooting or a natural disaster—the survivors have the hard job of putting their lives back together. We are changed, but life does go on. Marjorie has advice for survivors everywhere:

I think one thing to keep in mind is this is not going to define who they are. Even though right now it feels like this is their whole world and it just came crashing down and their lives are shattered, they are going to go to lunch again one day and laugh with their friends and not think about this. And they're going to get through it, even though it's going to take some time. And they can't be mad at themselves if it takes six months, a year, five years, ten years, because everyone has their own pace in healing. But eventually, it will happen and if they keep that in mind, I think there's light at the end of the tunnel.

Chapter Three

THE VIRGINIA TECH MASSACRE: FINDING MEANING IN INSANITY

On April 16, 2007, Seung-Hui Cho opened fire on the Virginia Tech campus in Blacksburg, Virginia. By the time he stopped shooting, thirty-three people were dead, including Cho, and many others were wounded.

COLIN GODDARD'S STORY

Twenty-one-year–old Colin Goddard's day had begun like any other, though he'd over-slept that morning. He was late to his nine-o'clock French class, but by 9:45, the morning had settled into its normal routine. Then, as he sat at his desk, he heard *pop! pop! pop!* "All semester we've heard loud noises and bang-ing" from a nearby construction site, Colin told the *USA Today* reporter. The teacher was

A picture (taken on a cell phone) from classroom 212 in Holden Hall, on the campus of Virginia Tech, where students hide during the shooting.

worried, but "when we heard it, we assured her it was just hammering."

Their professor wasn't reassured, however. She looked out into the hall, then came quickly back. "When she closed the door she was very terrified," Colin said. "She told us to call 911, told us to get to the ground. That was the last time I saw her."

Colin dialed 911, but the dispatcher couldn't hear him; she kept asking where he was located. Before Colin could get his message across, bullets splintered the wooden door beside him, and Cho pushed his way inside. Colin dropped the phone and hid beneath his desk.

From his hiding place, he saw a man wearing greenish pants, a white shirt, heavy boots, and pistol harnesses on each arm.

Colin couldn't see the man's face, only his body from the shoulders down. Without a word, the man walked up and down the aisles, firing a gun as he went. When he came to the desk where Colin was hiding, the man shot a bullet that went in Colin's knee and came out through his thigh. "I was very alert and conscious throughout the whole thing," Colin told *USA Today*. "It was terrifying," he said. To his surprise, though, it didn't hurt as much as he'd expected it would. "It felt like a big push of air and then a sting."

Why Did He Do It?

Two days after the massacre, NBC news received a package from the shooter, time-stamped between the first and second shooting episodes. It contained an 1,800-word essay, photos, and twenty-seven digitally recorded videos, in which Cho compared himself to Jesus Christ. He said, "You forced me into a corner and gave me only one option. . . You just loved to crucify me. You loved inducing . . . terror in my heart and ripping my soul all this time."

The Virginia Tech review panel concluded that because of Cho's inability to handle stress and the "frightening prospect" of being "turned out into the world of work, finances, responsibilities, and a family," Cho chose to engage in a fantasy where "he would be remembered as the savior of the oppressed, the downtrodden, the poor, and the rejected." The panel added, "His thought processes were so distorted that he began arguing to himself that his *evil* plan was actually doing good. His destructive fantasy was now becoming an obsession."

Then, still without speaking, the gunman was gone. Inside the room, the silence was broken by the sounds of whimpering. Someone made a gurgling sound. Nobody moved. Ten minutes later, the shooter was back.

Once again he walked up and down the aisles, shooting as he walked. Colin heard him reloading quickly between clips. As the gunman feet moved closer to Colin, Colin shut his eyes, pretending to be dead. Apparently, the shooter didn't care: he shot two more bullets into him.

Afterward, Colin heard one or two more shots—and then silence. Finally, after minutes had gone by, he cautiously raised his head. Next to him, his friend Kristina was trying to get to her feet, though she had been shot in the back. "Is he here?" Colin asked her. "Do you see anybody?"

"No," she answered, "I don't see him."

They heard the police outside the door, trying to open it, but a body blocked it. Someone in the room, the only person who hadn't been shot, got up and dragged the body out of the way. When the police burst into the room, they instantly shouted, "Shooter down! Shooter down!"

Colin may have been one of the last who were shot before Cho killed himself. Of the eighteen people who were in French class with him that day, only one came out unwounded; twelve died, including their teacher. Colin had survived the actual shoot-

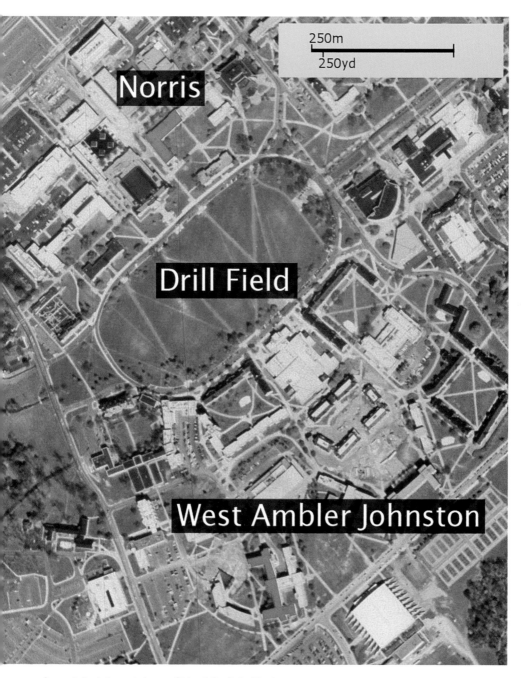

250m

250yd

Norris

Drill Field

West Ambler Johnston

An arial picture taken of the Virginia Tech campus
highlighting the two halls where the shooting took place,
in Norris and West Ambler Johnston Hall.

What Is Post-Traumatic Stress Disorder?

According to the National Institute of Mental Health:

Post-traumatic stress disorder (PTSD) develops after a terrifying ordeal that involved physical harm or the threat of physical harm. The person who develops PTSD may have been the one who was harmed, the harm may have happened to a loved one, or the person may have witnessed a harmful event that happened to loved ones or strangers.

PTSD was first brought to public attention in relation to war veterans, but it can result from a variety of traumatic incidents, such as mugging, rape, torture, being kidnapped or held captive, child abuse, car accidents, train wrecks, plane crashes, bombings, or natural disasters such as floods or earthquakes.

People with PTSD may startle easily, become emotionally numb (especially in relation to people with whom they used to be close), lose interest in things they used to enjoy, have trouble feeling affectionate, be irritable, become more aggressive, or even become violent. They avoid situations that remind them of the original incident, and anniversaries of the incident are often very difficult. PTSD symptoms seem to be worse if the event that triggered them was deliberately initiated by another person, as in a mugging or a kidnapping. Most people with PTSD repeatedly relive the trauma in their thoughts during the day and in nightmares when they sleep. These are called flashbacks. Flashbacks may consist of images, sounds, smells, or feelings, and are often triggered by ordinary occurrences, such as a door slamming or a car backfiring on the street. A person having a flashback may lose touch with reality and believe that the traumatic incident is happening all over again.

Not every traumatized person develops full-blown or even minor PTSD. Symptoms usually begin within 3 months of the incident but occasionally emerge years afterward. They must last more than a month to be considered PTSD. The course of the illness varies. Some people recover within 6 months, while others have symptoms that last much longer. In some people, the condition becomes chronic.

PTSD affects about 7.7 million American adults, but it can occur at any age, including childhood. . . . Certain kinds of medication and certain kinds of psychotherapy usually treat the symptoms of PTSD very effectively.

ing, but the long slow, recovery process had only just begun.

DEREK O'DELL'S STORY

Like Colin, Derek O'Dell is a Virginia Tech survivor—and he knows that survival is not an easy business. His wounds were minor, and three hours after the shooting, Derek was out of the hospital being interviewed on national television. A year later, however, when the month of April returns with its dogwood blossoms and sunshine, it fills him with anxiety. The spring air makes him feel as though something bad is going to happen.

Derek has post-traumatic stress disorder. Loud noises make him jump, and he smells gunpowder in his sleep. He sleeps with his door locked, he scans crowded rooms for both danger and escape routes.

Derek was sitting in German class when Seung-Hui Cho flung open the door and began shooting. The professor dropped to the floor. Students in the front row fell next. The friend sitting next to Derek was shot in the face. Hiding beneath the desks, Derek crawled to the back of the classroom.

He realized the shooter had left the room, though the door to the hallway stood open. Blood was everywhere, soaking the back-packs, the books, and the bodies that were tumbled across the room. He tasted gun-powder in his mouth and tried to think what to do.

Virginia Tech students mourn at a ceremony held on Tuesday,
April 17, the day after the shooting on the campus.

"When I heard shots in the hall, that jump-started me," he told a reporter from the *Washington Post*. He ran to shut the door, then called 911 on his cell phone. On the other side of the door, the gunman had returned. He pushed the door open enough to stick the barrel of his gun through it. Derek and some of the other students who were conscious shoved back until the door went shut again. Bullets splintered the wood, wounding Derek, and then the shooter retreated.

As the first of the injured students to be released from the hospital, Derek was swamped by reporters, wanting to hear what had happened. Derek took comfort in

bearing witness to the horrible events he had seen. "When I told my story, that became my numbing," he told the *Washington Post*.

But as the days went by, and then the weeks and months, Derek began to question himself. His doubts stripped him of any comfort. "I heard those shots. I had all that time to react. Forty-five seconds. Why didn't I do something . . . instead of hiding under the desk and crawling away? Encounter him when he first came in, I don't know, throw a book at him . . ."

Like the survivors of Columbine's shootings, Derek's family knows that there's no going back to the way life used to be. His

Virginia Tech students remember the victims of the shooting at a candlelight vigil held on April 17, 2007, the day after the shooting took place.

Virginia Tech English professor and poet Nikki Giovanni cheers, "We are the Hokies! We will prevail! We will prevail! We are Virginia Tech!" at a rally to remember the victims of the shooting.

mom told the *Washington Post*, "I don't know if anyone believes in closure. We're all living with this forever."

"People would call and ask are things back to normal yet," Derek's dad added. "I'd think, 'Of course not. It's never going to be normal again.'"

Being a survivor brought fame to Derek. The December after the massacre, *GQ* magazine flew him and his girlfriend to Los Angeles for a celebrity-studded party. Derek was one of the magazine's "Men of the Year," with a full-page portrait beneath the headline, followed by an article praising his bravery as a "Lifesaver."

But Derek didn't feel like a hero. In his mind, the heroes from that day were people like Liviu Librescu, the seventy-six-year–old Holocaust survivor who had been killed while holding his classroom door shut as he urged his students to leap out the window. Or Ryan Clark, the honors student who died when he went to check on what turned out to be Cho's first shot fired that morning.

But the rest of the world wanted Derek to be a hero too, whether he thought he was or not. He and the other survivors were invited backstage at a Dave Matthews concert. They were a stop on the presidential campaign trail. Bill Clinton met with them.

Derek's reaction to all the attention? "I want to be a person, not this victim." For Derek, being a survivor means learning how to become the person he's meant to be.

SURVIVOR GUILT

Derek's feelings of guilt and responsibility are not unusual reactions to the trauma he experienced. Psychologists tell us that after traumatic events, many people are troubled by the fact that they were unable to do more during the events. They could not take control over what was happening. R. J. Lifton, a psychologist, described this process:

> At the time of the trauma, there is a quick and immediate sense that one should respond according to one's ordinary standards, in certain constructive ways, by halting the path of the trauma or evil, or by helping other people in a

At the opening football game of the 2007 season, 32 orange balloons were released in remembrance of the victims of the Virginia Tech shooting.

constructive way. Neither of these may be possible during extreme trauma. At the very most, the response that is possible is less than the ideal expectation. . . . The response to this incomplete enactment can be perpetual self-condemnation. . . . The recovery process involves transcending that traumatized self.

ideal: the best possible condition.

enactment: acting, carrying out.

self-condemnation: blaming one's self.

transcending: existing above or apart from something.

chaotic: confused and disordered.

After a terrifying tragedy like the one that happened at Virginia Tech, life may seem random and chaotic, without meaning. Feeling guilty is a way of saying, *I could have changed all that if only I had done the right thing.* In other words, it's putting the blame on ourselves, rather than accepting a crazy world that scares us stiff.

But just as Derek O'Dell was not to blame for the actions of Seung-Hui Cho, nor could Derek have prevented them, so each of us must work through the various things in our own lives that shake our sense of who we are in relation to the world around us. Many people turn to religion as a way to find life's deeper meaning. Others seek out meaning within themselves or from their relationships with others. Some people turn to art and creativity as a way to handle their anxiety constructively. Many people use all three approaches.

Each individual is different, but all have one thing in common: to be a true survivor, we must be willing to go deeper, to move beyond our more shallow childhood view of

Social worker Kathleen Nader offers these steps for dealing with survivor guilt:

- **Thank goodness, you survived!**
  - –More people than you know are happy that you survived.
  - –Even if the rest of your life seems insignificant to you, we are relieved that you are alive.
- **Know that there is no offense in surviving.**
  - –It is good to survive.
  - –It is okay to delight in being alive.
- **Feel free to reassess your life.**
  - –Reassess what is valuable to you.
  - –Make the best of your life.
  - –Making the best of your life can be a tribute to your survival and to those who died.
  - –Take the opportunity to reevaluate the meaning of your life.
  - –Is your life all it can be?
  - –What is or can be your purpose? Your talent? Your benefit to life?
  - –Put guilt to good use (allow it to motivate you to be and do more).
- **Cherish life.**
  - –Enjoy each day and each act of kindness.
  - –Treasure the best of each day and each person.
  - –Be aware of your physical mortality in good and positive ways.
- **Process the traumatic experience and its associated symptoms with appropriate assistance.**
  - –Recognize the reawakening of old issues; survival may have triggered old feelings of worthlessness or unworthiness.
  - –Talk to people you are close to and trust.
  - –Seek out a reputable therapist or counselor.

the world, and become connected to something bigger than our own selfish desires. The world has always been a crazy and frightening place. And there have always been human beings who have risen to the challenge and created meaning in the midst of insanity.

President Bush attends the ceremony held the day after the shooting at Virginia Tech. Here, the President shakes hands with student government president James Tyger.

Chapter Four

SURVIVING BULLYING: YOU ARE NOT ALONE

bul ■ ly ■ ing: (noun) A deliberate, repeated, or long-term exposure to negative acts performed by a person or a group of persons of higher status or greater strength than the target.

Not all school violence is as severe as what took place at Columbine High School and Virginia Tech. Bullying is the kind of the violence that doesn't often make the headlines. It's **chronic** and ongoing, like a **low-grade** infection that never goes away. People may not lose their lives as a result of bullying—but they often lose their self-esteem and peace of mind. And the scars may last a lifetime.

chronic: continuing for a long time.

low-grade: of less intensity, quality, or degree.

MEGGIE ALFRED'S STORY

On a sunny day in late September, twelve-year-old Meggie Alfred was walking home from school when a group of boys from her school came up behind her on the sidewalk. She recognized them: they were the popular boys who played on the sports teams, the boys who everyone seemed to like. Meggie expected them to go on by her—they'd never paid any attention to her before—but then she heard them calling her name and laughing.

"Hey, Alfred," said a boy named Jerry Baldwin, "why are you wearing clothes that look like a four-year-old's?"

The other boys laughed. Meggie kept walking and tried to look like she hadn't

Not all bullying includes physical violence. Verbal bullying can be just as painful and humiliating.

heard, but the boys were on both sides of her now, keeping pace with her.

"Her clothes may look like a little kid's," said another boy, Adam Cobin, "but look at her boobs. Those are no four-year-old's."

This time the boys laughed harder. Meggie's pace quickened. Her face burned with mortification, but she kept her eyes straight ahead.

"Do you wear a bra, Meggie?" Jerry asked.

Meggie felt a hand grope over her back, fingers plucking at her skin through her shirt.

"Nope, no bra."

Suddenly, the boys were in front of her, pushing her back against the wall of the empty building on the corner near her house. A boy named George Clute stepped up so close to her she could smell his breath, and then his fingers fumbled over her breasts. His hands were covered with mud and left dark streaks across her pink shirt.

"Why are you shaking, Meggie?" Jerry was laughing.

"Are you excited, Meggie?" whispered George.

She shoved past them, her heart pounding in her ears, and tried to run down the sidewalk, away from them. Only a few more feet to her driveway, to safety. . . .

"Hey, not so fast!" A hand grabbed her, then set her flying into the street. She fell, scraping both knees, but she got up instantly.

As she ran the last few steps to her door, she could hear the boys still laughing behind her

Inside the house, her father was getting ready to go to work for his second-shift job. He looked up at her as she came in, her shirt dirty, her knees bloody. "What happened? You okay?"

"I'm fine," Meggie mumbled. "I just tripped and fell."

HOW FEAR LEADS TO ISOLATION

Like many victims of bullying, Meggie was afraid to tell her parents what had happened. She knew her parents wouldn't be with her in the hallway at school or on the way home—and if she got the bullies in trouble, sooner or later, they would take their revenge. The fear of being attacked, combined with her sense of shame and embarrassment over the things the boys said and did to her, pushed Meggie into a secret prison where she didn't dare ask for help.

She was afraid to go to school now, for fear she would encounter the boys during her walk there. At school, she avoided the hallways where she knew the boys would be. Once, they caught her on the stairwell and dropped her books over the railing, then laughed as she scrambled down the stairs to pick up her scattered textbooks and papers. Another time, they tripped her as she was getting her lunch in the cafeteria, spilling chicken noodle soup in a greasy arc across her sweater. She dreaded coming home, for fear they'd grab her on the sidewalk again, so she found reasons to stay after school, working in the library or asking for help from her math teacher, waiting until the boys would most likely be somewhere else.

Meggie started making up reasons to stay home from school as much as she could. Most of the time, she didn't really need to make up anything: her stomach really did seem to hurt most of the time. At night,

Kids get bullied for many reasons: because they're smarter—or less intelligent than others; because they're heavier—or smaller than others; because they dress differently, speak differently, or act differently.

In 2005, a multinational study funded by the World Health Organization (WHO) and managed by the European Public Health Association found that severe bullying causes physical and psychological symptoms of distress.

The physical symptoms identified by the study were:	The psychological symptoms identified were:
headache	bad temper, feeling "out of sorts"
stomachache	
backache	nervousness
dizziness	sadness
morning tiredness	difficulties in getting to sleep
	feeling left out, loneliness
	helplessness

she had nightmares and woke up feeling exhausted. Her life had turned into gauntlet of dangers she was forced to run every day she went to school. Her grades dropped. The only times she was happy were on weekends and vacation days, when she refused to leave her house. This went on for years, until she was in high school, when suddenly the boys seemed to lose interest in tormenting her.

Through it all, Meggie had felt as though she were alone, isolated from her family and from the other students at her school. She believed she was the only one who had to endure such pain and embarrassment, that there was something wrong with her that had brought it on her. In fact, however, around the world, many people have shared her experiences, or something a lot like them.

According to the U.S. National Institutes of Health, at least one in every seven young people has experienced some form of bullying. Other studies show nearly one-third of young people are bullied at least once a month—and that 60 percent of U.S. teens witness bullying at least once a day. Many students report harassment or bullying on school property because of their race, ethnicity, religion, gender, sexual orientation, or disability. These kids probably all felt a lot like Meggie did, frightened and isolated. Some of them have used the Internet as an outlet for their emotions.

BULLYING STORIES FROM THE INTERNET

A girl named Rosie wrote:

> It began when I was about 5 years old I suppose. On the first day of school, I was so scared of all the people I began to cry, all the other kids laughed and from then on everyone seemed to hate me. I've never fully understood why, the only reason was that I was shy. I don't understand how people can be so cruel to someone just because they are shy. Of course there were other reasons, I'm an ugly, disgusting and unlovable person all round, or so I believe now, because

According to a recent study (2004) done by the University of Texas at Austin, Children bullied for the first time before they hit puberty seem to get over it, but those who are victimized for the first time later on in puberty seem to become more aggressive or are more likely to turn to drink as a means of coping.

of all that happened to me. During the first few years of school I never really had a friend and people just left me out of things and called me horrible names. It got worse when a new girl came to the school during the last 3 or 4 years that I was there. Her, and two other girls were the main people who bullied me, although everyone else did join frequently, it's those three who I really remember.

Another young person shared a similar story:

After this girl came I was never left alone. I stood next to the school doors in the same place every day, and I have never felt so alone in all my life. I stood every day, watching everybody else playing and laughing, just waiting for when they would all come and stand around me to laugh at me and call me names. I wanted to die then, I thought of killing myself all the time just to get out of school, I'm not sure why I never just did it. Inside school, in the classroom, I had to sit at a table with the people who bullied me and I just sat and listened to them being cruel to me, they never stopped, it honestly was constant.

They threw things at me, stole my things, tripped me up, but it only ever once got properly physical, I was grabbed, thrown around and my ankle was very nearly broken—people just stood and laughed. The worst thing, though, was being left out, having to watch everyone else playing. I did try to join in but I was always rejected so

Bullying is more emotionally damaging to teens than to younger children.

Daily Bus Bullying

12 million students
are bullied on the school bus each day.
Bullying can be words or actions.

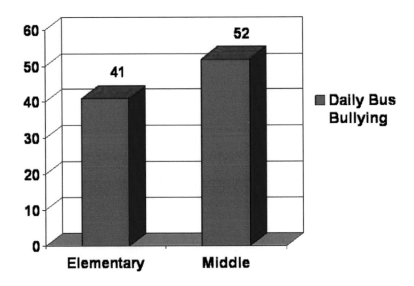

Source: Kamaron Foundation Student and Adult Surveys

© 2006 Kamaron Institute

In 2006, the Kamaron Institute found that school buses are a common location for bullying to take place.

I think I just gave up in the end. Sometimes if someone was alone they would ask me to play with them, but I was always the last resort, and often the only reason someone asked me was so that they could take me to their group and leave me out and call me names. This happened for years and I'd rather die than ever have to go through all that again, it was a living hell. I don't really know what else to say about what happened, I have never spoken about it and writing this short story was very hard. I remember all that happened, not the words, but their faces, how I felt, how I felt inside. It killed me, and I still don't think I realize the full impact it has had on me.

Please, if anyone else is going through this I want to talk to you, to help. The thought of this happening to other people hurts me so very much. I never told a soul, there was no one to tell and perhaps if I had shared it things would have been different. It hurts so much to keep it all inside and people being bullied shouldn't have to do that.

And one more story from the Internet:

Bullying has been a big part of my life. I'm not sure why people do it, all I know is that they do and it hurts. I can't

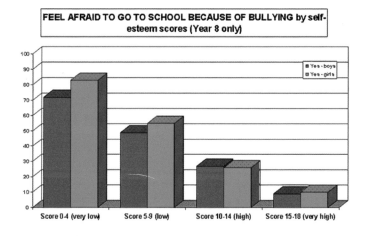

FEEL AFRAID TO GO TO SCHOOL BECAUSE OF BULLYING by self-esteem scores (Year 8 only)

Bullying is an international problem. A UK-survey found that children with low self-esteem scores are more apt to be afraid to go to school because of the bullying they face there.

This graph shows the percentages of Canadian students in each grade who participated in bullying in the past two months. Except for grade nine, an age when girls are apparently more likely than at any other time to be bullies, boys are far more likely to be bullies than girls are.

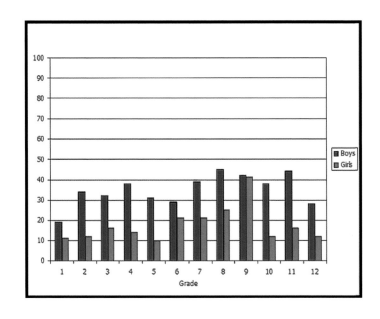

actually remember a time without being teased. I used to have such a big heart, and laughed freely. But then when I was picked on, I slowly set myself away from the outside world. Nobody liked me and nobody cared, is what I often thought. Now that I think about it, the early years of being bullied weren't as bad as how it is now. Through the years the names progressed, I became a loner, and someone to pick on. This past 7th grade was the hardest on me so far, I guess. I got in a few fights, have been called names, and got to an all time low. I didn't trust anybody really, and I was actually bitten by a "friend" just so she could have her way. I was treated like dirt actually, no, probably lower that dirt because I wasn't popular, or skinny,

The Long-Terms Effects of Bullying

It is not necessary to be physically harmed in order to suffer lasting harm. Words and gestures are quite enough. In fact, the old saying, "Sticks and stones may break my bones but names will never harm me: is more or less exactly backwards. For the most part, physical damage sustained in a fistfight heals readily, especially damage that is sustained during the resilient childhood years. What is far more difficult to mend is the primary wound that bullying victims suffer which is damage to their self-concepts; to their identities. Bullying is an attempt to instill fear and self-loathing. Being the repetitive target of bullying damages your ability to view yourself as a desirable, capable and effective individual.

There are two ugly outcomes that stem from learning to view yourself as a less than desirable, incapable individual. The first ugly outcome is that it becomes more likely that you will become increasingly susceptible to becoming depressed and/or angry and/or bitter. Being bullied teaches you that you are undesirable, that you are not safe in the world, and (when it is dished out by forces that are physically superior to yourself) that you are relatively powerless to defend yourself. When you are forced, again and again, to contemplate your relative lack of control over the bullying process, you are being set up for Learned Helplessness (e.g., where you come to believe that you can't do anything to change your ugly situation even if that isn't true), which in turn sets you up for hopelessness and depression.

At the same time, you may be learning that you are helpless and hopeless, you are also learning how you are seen by bullies, which is to say, you are learning that you are seen by others as weak, pathetic, and a loser. And, by virtue of the way that identity tends to work, you are being set up to believe that these things the bullies are saying about you are true.

(*Source:* Dr. Michael Dombeck, MentalHelp.net, www.mentalhelp.net/poc/view_doc.php?type=doc&id=13057)

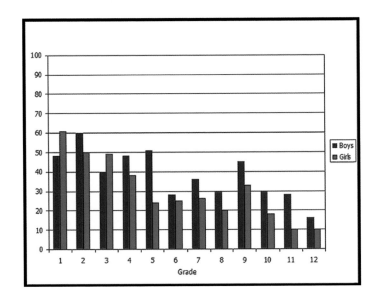

A Canadian study indicates that in the upper grades, girls are less apt to be bullied than boys are.

or any of that. The only thing that kept me up was writing, art and some of the best teachers in the world.

I used to cry sometimes because it got so bad, and crying is something I've tried to push out. I don't deserve to cry, is what I told myself. I was called fat, . . . a nobody, a geek, and just about anything else you can name. I was even made fun of on the last day of school! The only thing that kept me, again, from sinking down further into depression were some teachers.

WHAT SCARS DOES BULLYING LEAVE?

Psychologists have linked bullying to a variety of emotional and physical disorders.

Kids who are bullied often suffer from poor self-concepts. They frequently experience depression and anxiety disorders. They seem to be especially prone to eating disorders, which can run the gamut from anorexia to obesity. And most tragically of all, kids who have been bullied are far more likely to commit suicide.

But being bullied doesn't mean you're doomed to be a failure in life. Just as the survivors of the Columbine shootings and the Virginia Tech massacre are finding ways to put their lives back together, so have many people who were the victims of bullying. Some of these people have even gone on to become famous.

anorexia: a disorder involving a distorted body image, in which a person is extremely afraid of being overweight and tries to lose weight by excessive dieting and exercise, and often by self-induced vomiting or other means.

CHRISTINA AGUILERA

Christina always knew she wanted to spend her life singing, and she had plenty of talent to go along with her ambition. But that didn't mean she was immune to bullying.

As a child, she lined up her toys as her audience and sang to them; when she got a little older, she performed in talent competitions, defeating her opponents with little effort. Meanwhile, though, her class-

mates at school were jealous of her celebrity, and began teasing her, isolating her and even trying to physically assault her. At her senior prom, when a DJ played her hit single "Genie in a Bottle," most of her classmates stopped dancing and left the floor. They even went as far as vandalizing her family's property and slashing the tires on the family car. To escape the harassment, Christina and her family relocated to a new neighborhood. At her new school, she refused to talk about her talent for fear she would face the same kind of negative attention.

Today, if you had the chance to meet Christina, you'd probably never suspect she had gone through any kind of bullying when she was younger. She has had four number-one singles on the Billboard Top 100 and two top-five albums in the United States; she's also won three Grammy Awards and one Latin Grammy Award.

But Christina isn't only successful professionally. She also works hard to be a positive force for good in the world around her. The Women's Center & Shelter of Greater Pittsburgh receives financial support from Christina, and she is also affiliated with PETA, the Wildlife Foundation, and the Coalition for the Cure of Blindness. At her November 2006 wedding, Aguilera and husband Jordan Bratman donated all of their wedding gifts to charities in support of Hurricane Katrina victims.

TIGER WOODS

As a child of mixed race (he calls himself "Cablinasian," a mixture of Caucasian, black, American Indian, and Asian), other kids didn't know how to categorize Tiger—they just knew he was "different." On his first day of kindergarten, a group of older boys tied Tiger to a tree and taunted him with racial insults. Life didn't get a whole lot easier for Tiger; a serious stuttering problem brought him even more negative attention and harassment.

Despite all that, Tiger was a good student, who went on to study at Stanford University. Today, Tiger is considered to be one of the greatest golfers of all time, second only to the legendary Jack Nicklaus. Tiger has had more wins on the PGA tour than any other current golfer. In 2006, Tiger was named *Forbes'* highest-paid athlete, and he ranks second on the list of overall highest-paid celebrities, making around $87 million a year.

But even more important, Tiger is doing what he can to give back to the world. He's established several charitable projects, including the Tiger Woods Foundation (a child-focused organization that offers golf clinics to disadvantaged children, university scholarships, grant programs, and much more), Tiger Woods Learning Center (a learning center with multimedia facilities, plus summer and community outreach programs), Tiger Jam (an annual fundraising concert), and Target World Challenge (an annual off-season charity golf tournament, in which he donates all of his winnings to his foundation). After the 2004 tsunami, Tiger used his foundation to reach out to the people who had lost so much in the tsunami.

BILL CLINTON

Former president Clinton wasn't always a charming and charismatic politician. He used

to be an overweight little boy who faced teasing at school. The brunt of "fat jokes," he struggled with his body image. He used books and music as an escape (he loved playing the saxophone so much he considered becoming a professional musician), and he excelled at school.

In 1992, at the age of forty-six, he became

one of the youngest presidents in American history. Despite the **controversies** and scandals that plagued his years in office, President Clinton led the United States into years of economic health and growth. In his post-presidential career, he's continued to work for others through the Clinton Foundation. This organization is working to improve economies around the world; it's tackled HIV/AIDS as one of its major efforts; it's fighting to building a healthier environment; and it's leading a campaign to end childhood obesity (after all, Bill Clinton knows firsthand

controversies: disputes, disagreements.

the emotional and physical challenges these kids face).

CHRIS ROCK

When Chris Rock was a kid, his parents worried about the education he'd receive in the neighborhood school—so they had him bused to an almost all-white high school in Bensonhurst, a white neighborhood in Brooklyn known at the time for its poor race relations. There, Chris faced constant bullying, just because he was black. Years later, he remembered, "I got beat up just about every day. . . . I got kicked and whatever."

Today, Chris has turned the memories from those painful years into a popular sitcom—*Everybody Hates Chris*—that is loosely based

on his childhood experiences. The *New York Times* recently referred to Chris as "probably the funniest and smartest comedian working today." *Entertainment Weekly* voted him funniest person in America, and Comedy Central's 100 Greatest Stand-Ups of All Time ranked him number 5 on the 2004 list. His jokes typically focus on race relations in the United States. He may still be angry at the treatment he received—but he's managed to turn that anger into entertainment and a successful career.

HARRISON FORD

In high school, Harrison Ford was a shy and awkward loner. His peers harassed him constantly, and even voted him the student "least

likely to succeed." For years, Harrison silently endured the taunting and abuse—until one day he snapped and beat up one of the bullies.

He managed to survive high school and went on to college, where he took some drama classes. After graduation, he supported himself doing carpentry work—and a man named George Lucas just happened to hire him to build some cabinets in his house. Mr. Lucas was looking for an actor to play in American Graffiti . . . and Harrison's life changed forever.

Today, you'd never guess that Harrison Ford could have ever been the kid no one liked. He has starred in twenty-seven movies, which have grossed more than $3.3 billion at the box office. *People Magazine* once named him as one of the "50 Most Beautiful People in the World," as well as the "Sexiest Man Alive." But more important, Harrison is passionate about protecting our planet's environment, and in 2002, he was presented with the Global Environmental Citizen Award.

WINONA RYDER

effeminate: having characteristics or mannerisms generally considered feminine.

When Winona was ten years old, her family moved to Petaluma, California. During her first week there, she was harassed by a group of kids who mistook her for "an **effeminate**, scrawny boy." The bullying was so bad that her parents eventually pulled her out of school; Winona was home schooled for the rest of that year, and she began taking acting lessons at the American Conservatory Theater in San Francisco. Eventually, though, she graduated from Petaluma High School with a straight-A average.

Winona has had her share of troubles over the years, and no doubt some of the scars she bears came from the bullying she received as a kid. Despite that, today she's considered one of Hollywood's most beautiful and successful actors. A Golden Globe winner and two-time Academy Award nominee, Winona has performed in more than thirty films over her twenty-year career.

And Winona has also gone on to be an **activist** who speaks out for others. She dedicated her film *Little Women* to Polly Klaas, a young girl from her hometown of Petaluma who was kidnapped and murdered; Winona offered a $200,000 reward for anyone who had any information regarding Klaas' death, and is a supporter of the Polly Klaas foundation. She is also on the Board of American Indian College Funds.

activist: a person who actively promotes a cause, especially a political cause.

EVA LONGORIA

When Eva was growing up in Corpus Christi, Texas, she was teased for being ugly. The other kids called her names like "Ugly Girl" and "Morena Fea," which means "ugly dark girl" in Spanish.

Eva might have believed her tormentors and decided she was truly ugly—but instead, she grew up to become one of *People en Español*'s "50 Most Beautiful"; according to *Maxim*, she is the "#1 Hottest Woman in the World." Recently, she signed an exclusive worldwide contract as the newest face of L'Oreal. But Eva is far more than just a pretty face. She also enjoys reading and studying science, and she's proven her talent as an actor. In 2005, she and her co-stars for the hit TV show *Desperate Housewives* won the Screen Actors' Guild Award for Best Television Ensemble, Comedy. She was also nominated for the 2005 Golden Globe for her role in the TV show, and she's moved into film acting as well.

STEVEN SPIELBURG

When Steven was a teenager, his family moved from Phoenix, Arizona, to Saratoga, California. The kids at Saratoga High School picked on the new kid for being Jewish, for acting "weird," for not fitting in. As an adult, when Steven was asked about his experiences at Saratoga High School, he would always say that it was "hell on Earth."

Steven used his creativity to escape that hell. He made his first film when he was twelve, and he'd made at least four movies on his own by the time he was eighteen, including a 140-minute science fiction epic called *Firelight*. Today, he's a four-time Academy Award-winning director, who directed blockbuster hits like *Jaws, E.T., Saving Private Ryan, Schindler's List, Indiana Jones and the Temple of Doom*, and many more.

WHAT HAPPENED TO MEGGIE ALFRED?

Life got a little easier for Meggie Alfred as she grew older. In high school, she made a few close friends, including her English teacher, who encouraged her to pursue a career in writing. Meg majored in writing in college, then went on to get a journalism master's degree, and ended up writing children's books, using a **pseudonym**.

pseudonym: a false name, often used to disguise one's identity when writing.

Meg draws on her experiences as a child for the plots she writes. She still remembers what it felt like to be terrified to go to school, and that pain never quite dies. "There's a part of me that always wonders, Am I really good enough? Am I ugly? Am I

What Is Verbal Bullying?

- referring to the person by derogative nicknames
- mocking the person's appearance (facial features, physique, or clothes) in front of his/her peers
- mocking the person's style of talking
- making the person the "fall guy" of jokes
- telling the person that his or her close friends do not like him or her anymore
- making intimidating (anonymous) phone calls to the person
- threatening to humiliate the person if he or she will not hand over lunch money, etc.
- making negative comments about the person's intelligence
- verbal threats of physical harm to the person and/or his or her possessions, such as clothes, schoolbooks, locker items
- verbal threats of physical harm to the person's friends if they continue to be friends with the person

stupid? Will people find out the truth about me—and then will they stop liking me? No matter how old I get, I can't seem to get rid of those voices. Sometimes, I just want to curl up and eat cookies, the way I used to after school, to drown out the pain and self-doubt—and sometimes that's what I do. I blame my weight problem on those voices! But I'm not going to beat myself up over it. Because those voices have also fueled my talent as a writer. They've made me who I am, a storyteller who hopefully inspires other kids

Children who are bullied are more apt to have self-esteem issues. They may absorb the barrage of constant negative messages and believe there is something truly wrong with themselves.

to face their own bullies with courage and grace.

"I guess you'd say, I give myself a break when it comes to this—but it occurred to me recently, I'd never given that same break to the bullies from my childhood. I'd never really forgiven them for all the things they did and said. In my mind, they were still one-dimensional characters, the villains, the evil monsters, not human little boys."

Overcoming a Poor Self-Concept

Meggie Alfred and the celebrities whose stories we've included here share a few things in common: all of them were bullied as children—and all of them overcame their poor self-concepts (that taunting voice inside them that insisted they weren't good enough, pretty enough, or smart enough) by using their creativity to express themselves, as well as finding ways to give to others. Psychologists agree: creativity (whether it's making music, telling jokes, painting pictures, acting, or writing books) and generosity to others are two of the best ways to overcome a poor self-concept.

AND WHAT ABOUT THE BULLIES? DID THEY "SURVIVE"?

Recently, Meg Alfred decided she wanted to write a book from the other perspective: the bully's point of view. To do that, she needed to get inside a bully's head and understand what motivated him. She was also curious: Do bullies grow up and feel guilty for their actions? Or do they grow up to be adult bullies? She decided to track down the bullies she'd known in school and talk to them. In the process, she hoped to be able to forgive them for what they'd done.

She discovered that all three of the boys she remembered best still lived in the small city where they'd grown up; two of them even lived within a few blocks of their old school. When she called them, Jerry Baldwin and Adam Cobin were willing to meet with her, but George Clute refused.

"Do you remember being mean to me?" Meg asked Jerry when they met at a coffee shop.

He looked uncomfortable. "Yeah, I guess. Kids do that sort of thing, though, don't they? It's just part of growing up. My kids probably do the same thing." He shrugged and gave her a grin.

Jerry had once been considered the best-looking boy in the school, she remembered. Today, he was going bald and had a belly, but she could still see some of his old charm.

Still, she didn't return his smile. "I lived in terror of you boys," she told him. "You made my life miserable. What made you treat me that way?"

Jerry shrugged again and his smile faded. "It was just a joke, Meggie. We were just kidding around. Come on. We didn't really *do* anything. I mean, we never . . . it was just teasing. And we're all grown up now. You didn't come here to yell at me, did you, after all these years?" He tried his charming grin on her again.

"No," she said, still not smiling. "I didn't. I was just curious. I wanted to understand."

Jerry looked down at the table between them. He played with his coffee cup. "It was just what kids do, Meggie. We didn't mean anything by it."

Meg met with Adam Cobin next. She wondered if she would hear the same story from him as she had from Jerry, but as soon as she sat down with Adam in the coffee shop, he leaned across the table and said, "I'm really glad to see you. I've thought about you a lot."

She studied his face. He'd been a thin kid, and now he was a thin man, with a narrow face that looked as though it had smiled a lot over the years. She found herself thinking that if she'd just met him, she would like him. "You have?" she asked him.

"Yeah. I've wanted to apologize. We were such jerks to you. We . . ." He shook his head. "It's bothered me over the years, especially

Bullying has been a part of childhood for generation after generation. By bringing more attention to this problem, educators and lawmakers hope to finally decrease bullying and its consequences.

now I have kids of my own." He looked down at his hands, then glanced up at her and smiled. "We've got two boys and a little girl. If I ever caught my boys treating a girl the way we did you, they'd be in a big trouble. And if I ever caught anybody doing to my girl what we did . . . well, I'd probably knock their socks off. We teach our kids to respect others, that violence isn't the answer. But I'd have a hard time not slugging someone who

Younger, smaller kids are often the target of older, larger bullies.

bullied my little girl the way we did you."

"What do you think made you act that way when you were a kid?" Meg asked him. "Didn't your parents teach you the things you're teaching your kids?"

"No, they taught me. If my dad had known what I was doing, he would have paddled me. I'm sorry, Meg. It was just that I wanted Jerry to like me. He was popular, everyone liked him, and I was just this skinny little kid with no friends. Then Jerry took me under his wing, so I went along with everything he did. I tried to be just like him, so he'd like me, so everyone else would like me. I was an idiot, Meg. I hated myself even at the time, and when I got older, it really haunted me, some of the things we'd done to you and a couple of other kids." He held out his hand to her. "Can you forgive me?"

Meg hesitated, then took his hand. "Sure, Adam. I forgive you."

They ended up talking about a lot of things, sharing various things that had happened over the years since they'd left school.

As they stood up to leave, Meg asked, "So what about Jerry and George? Did you stay in touch?"

Adam shook his head. "Not really. It's a small community, though, so we all still know each other. Jerry's still the same old Jerry, easygoing, likeable, good-old-Jerry who gets along with everyone. I guess you probably never got to see that side of him, huh? I don't think he's big on thinking, though, if you know what I mean. It's probably never occurred to him how mean we were to you and some of the other kids."

"What about George?" Meg asked.

Adam shook his head. "George has been arrested a couple of times for beating up his wife. They're separated now, last I heard. George is a mean guy. He was mean when we were kids, and he's still mean."

"What do you think made him that way?"

Adam shrugged. "I couldn't say. Maybe some guys are like that. But his dad was just the same. Mr. Clute used to slap George's mom around right in front of us. And once or twice, George would come to school with bruises, where his dad had hit him the night before. I guess he was probably mad at the world—who wouldn't be, with a dad like that?—and he'd learned from his father that it's okay to take it out on people who are smaller."

Meg and Adam said good-bye, and Meg went home with lots of ideas for her book.

"I talked to some child psychologists, too," she said. "I found out that Jerry, Adam, and George were good examples of the reasons why kids bully. Like Adam, some of them do it because of peer pressure, because they want to be liked, to fit in. Maybe even to avoid being bullied themselves. Deep inside, they know better, and they feel guilty, but they go along with their peers. Others are more like Jerry: they have great self-concepts, but not

Teenage girls may not physically bully each other—but their own brand of bullying can be just as hurtful.

much empathy. It just never seems to occur to them that other people are real, that other people have feelings. Unlike Jerry, most of them eventually grow up and realize the truth. And then there are kids like George—kids who have been knocked around at home and are full of rage. So they take it out where it's safe: on someone smaller than themselves. And if they don't get help, they often grow up to repeat the pattern they learned at home."

CAN BULLYING BE STOPPED?

Bullying was once considered to be one of the normal hazards of childhood. Today, since the shootings at Columbine (where two kids who were bullied turned around and shot their classmates), school districts are taking bullying seriously. Anti-bullying programs begin at the earliest levels of elementary school. While school personnel enforce zero-tolerance policies for bullying, teachers also do their best to teach young people empathy, tolerance, and understanding.

Clearly, bullying is dangerous. Its damage can be long lasting (for both the person who was bullied and the bully himself), and it can even reach into the future and touch future generations. As educators, psychologists, and government leaders struggle to find ways to make schools safe from bullying, the violence continues to break out, putting students around the world at risk.

Sometimes, kids who are scared and angry may respond with extreme violence.

As each new violent incident occurs, parents and students feel a fresh sense of terror and outrage. It's tempting to think that if governments and school districts pass enough laws, if they're strict enough and careful enough, school violence will become a thing of the past. And when that doesn't happen, when instead some new horrendous shooting makes the headlines, it's only human to want to blame someone.

"It was easy for me to forgive Adam," Meg Alfred said, "and even George, once I knew his story. It was harder for me to forgive Jerry. I still find myself hating him. But I try to let it go. Forgiveness is good for you, for the world. That's what I believe anyway."

A small Amish community in Pennsylvania agrees with Meg. When school violence tore apart their families, instead of focusing on their fear and anger, they focused on forgiveness.

Some suggestions from *Teen Touch* (www.teentouch.org) for coping with bullying:

- Check to see if your school has anti-bullying guidelines or some kind of rules about bullying. Then, follow the guidelines.
- Tell a friend what is happening and ask for help. It'll be harder for the bully to pick on you if you have a friend with you.
- Bullies usually pick on kids who are alone. Lonely kids are often targets. Find friends and allies. It's harder to be a bully in front of a group.
- Sometimes, if more than one person is being bullied by the same person, these people will hang around together, so that it's harder for the bully to pick on one person. (Sometimes there's safety in numbers.)
- If a group is bullying you, look the weakest one in the eye and say, "This isn't funny," and then walk away. Or, you can ask one of the group members when they're alone why the group finds it necessary to gang up on one person.
- Try to ignore the bully, or say, "No" strongly, then turn and walk away. Don't worry if people think you're running away. Just remember that it's hard for the bully to continue bullying someone who isn't there.
- Try not to show that the bully has upset you–the bully may get bored if there's no reaction coming from you. They can't bully you if you don't care.
- Don't fight back if you can help it. This could make the situation worse, you could get hurt, or you could get blamed for starting the trouble.

- It's not worth getting hurt just to hang on to your possessions or money. If you feel threatened, give the bullies what they want. Property can be replaced; you can't.
- Believe in yourself. Don't believe what the bully says. You know that's not true.
- Check your body language—if you stoop, hang your head and hunch over, you may be giving off "victim" signals.
- Try to use humor to disarm the bully—the important thing is to say something confidently back to the bully.
- Avoid places where bullying is likely to occur.
- Tell the bully how the bullying is affecting you.
- Tell a friend, a parent, teacher, an adult or other person in authority. If you're too nervous, take along a friend for moral support.
- Use assertiveness skills: ask questions; change the subject; agree with the bully; ask for advice; paraphrase the bully's comments; set limits.
- Sign up for self-defense courses, because they'll give you more confidence.
- These lessons don't mean that you should fight back, but they do make you feel more confident.
- Sometimes asking the bully to repeat what was said can put them off. Some bullies aren't brave enough to repeat the remark, so they tone it down or drop it. If they repeat it, you've made them do something they hadn't planned on, and gives you some control.
- Keep a diary of what's happening. You may need a written record of proof.
- **REMEMBER:** telling about bullying is not "telling tales." You have the right to be safe from attacks and harassment. Even if the bully finds out, it is better to have things in the open.

Chapter Five

VIOLENCE IN A ONE-ROOM SCHOOLHOUSE: THE POWER OF FORGIVENESS

On a quiet October morning in Pennsylvania's Lancaster County, Emma Mae Zook was teaching her class. The Amish students at the West Nickel Mines one-room schoolhouse ranged in age from young children to teenagers. They all looked up when a man came in the building, mumbling something they couldn't understand. Many of the children may have recognized him as the man who drove the milk truck that stopped each day at their farms. The man went outside, then came back. This time he carried a 9mm handgun in his hand.

The man—whom the world would later learn was Charles Carl Roberts—told the boys in the classroom to help him unload his pickup truck. Emma Mae took the opportunity to escape and run for help. When Roberts saw her leave, he ordered one of the boys to stop

Although there was no phone in the schoolhouse, Emma Mae Zook knew that the nearby farm would have a phone where she could call for help. The Amish do not have phones inside their homes, but they do use phones when needed. This farmer has provided an outside phone booth for his Amish neighbors to use.

her and threatened to shoot everyone if their teacher got away. Emma Mae had already reached a nearby farm, however, where she asked Amos Smoker to call 911.

Who Are the Amish?

The community of Nickel Mines is Old Order Amish, a group whose roots stretch back to the Anabaptist movement at the time of the Protestant Reformation in sixteenth-century Europe. In those days, the early forerunners of today's Amish were no strangers to violence: hundreds of Anabaptists were burned at the stake, decapitated, and tortured because they taught that individuals should have the freedom to make voluntary decisions about religion. This belief laid the foundation for our modern concepts of religious liberty and the separation of church and state.

Today, the Amish practice a lifestyle that is uniquely their own, one that sets them apart from the rest of the modern world. The rules of their church cover most aspects of day-to-day living: no power-line electricity, limiting the use of telephones, prohibition of ownership and operation of an automobile, and "plain" dress. The Amish seek to limit contact with the outside world; instead, they emphasize church and family relationships. Amish children attend Amish schools, one-room schoolhouses for children in grades one through eight. About 227,000 Amish currently live in the United States, mostly in Pennsylvania, Indiana, Ohio, and New York State. There are also Amish communities in Ontario, Canada.

Meanwhile, Roberts and the boys carried lumber, a shotgun, a stun gun, wires, chains, nails, tools, and a length of wooden board with multiple sets of metal eyehooks into the classroom. Then, Roberts barricaded the front door, and ordered the girls to line up against the chalkboard. He let a pregnant woman, three parents with babies, and all the

A typical one-room Amish schoolhouse in Lancaster County, Pennsylvania.

male students leave the building; one little girl also escaped: nine-year-old Emma Fisher who spoke only Pennsylvania German, and had not understood Robert's orders. That left ten girls inside with Roberts.

A few minutes later the state troopers arrived as Roberts was binding the arms and legs of his hostages with plastic ties. Roberts warned the troopers to leave immediately, threatening to shoot the girls if they didn't. The police officers backed away and used the loudspeakers in their cruisers to tell Roberts to throw out his weapons and exit the schoolhouse. Roberts refused, again ordering the officers to leave.

By 11:00 a.m. (only a half hour or so after Roberts had first entered the schoolhouse), a crowd that included police officers, emergency medical technicians, and residents of the village had gathered outside the schoolhouse.

Later, when they were finally safe, the survivors described what had been happening inside the building. The girls talked softly to each other. Two sisters, thirteen-year-old Marian and ten-year-old Barbie Fisher, asked that they be shot first and that the others be spared. When Roberts opened fire, Barbie was wounded, while her older sister was killed.

As soon as the troopers heard the gunfire, they ran toward the schoolhouse. As they reached the windows, the shooting abruptly stopped. Roberts had committed suicide.

The troopers broke down the door and carried out the girls. Ambulances and emergency medical technicians rushed to the scene, but three of the girls were already dead.

Two more died early the next morning, leaving five more in critical condition. The youngest victim was six years old, the oldest only thirteen. They had been shot at close range. Lancaster County's deputy **coroner** told the Washington Post that she had counted at least two-dozen bullet wounds in one child alone before she had to stop and ask a colleague to continue for her. Inside the school, she said, "there was not one desk, not one chair, in the whole schoolroom that was not splattered with either blood or glass. There were bullet holes everywhere, everywhere."

coroner: an official who investigates any death suspected of not being due to natural causes.

WHY DID ROBERTS DO IT?

Roberts's wife last saw him earlier that morning when they had walked their children to the bus stop. When Mrs. Roberts returned home from a prayer group a little before 11:00 a.m., she discovered four suicide notes; one was addressed to herself and one to each of their three children. Roberts called his wife from the schoolhouse on his cell phone and told her he had molested two young

Charles Carl Roberts

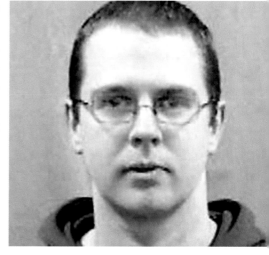

The Survivors of the Shooting at Nickel Mines Schoolhouse

Rosanna King, six years old. She was removed from life support and sent home to die at the request of her family, but she did survive. She had serious brain injuries and a year later still could not walk or talk—but family members said she recognized them and smiled frequently.

Rachel Ann Stoltzfus, eight years old.

Barbie Fisher, ten years old. She underwent repeated shoulder surgeries and healed enough to pitch for her school softball team.

Sarah Ann Stoltzfus, twelve years old. She lost part of the vision in her left eye.

Esther King, thirteen years old.

Those Who Lost Their Lives

Naomi Rose Ebersol, seven years old, died at the scene.

Marian Stoltzfus Fisher, thirteen years old, died at the scene.

Anna Mae Stoltzfus, twelve years old, was declared dead on arrival at the Lancaster Hospital.

Lena Zook Miller, seven years old, died the next day.

Mary Liz Miller, eight years old, died the next day.

female relatives twenty years ago (when he was twelve) and had been daydreaming about molesting again. Later, however, the two relatives told police that no such incident had ever happened—and Roberts did not molest any of the Amish girls.

Clearly, Roberts was a disturbed individual. The survivors from the schoolhouse said that before he opened fire, he told them, "I'm angry at God and I need to punish some Christian girls to get even with him. . . . I'm going to make you pay for my daughter."

A typical Amish home is like a step backward in time. They have no electricity, they heat their homes with wood, and they dress in simple dark-colored clothing without buttons or zippers.

displaced: directed toward an innocent or unrelated target as a substitute for the true source of an emotion.

(The Roberts's had had a baby daughter who died in 1997.) Later, a psychologist speculated that Roberts had been "sitting on a whole bunch of conflicting ideas about how to make things right with the world." She went on to say that the Amish community's "simplicity and devoutness" may have triggered "**displaced** rage" in Roberts, or "made him feel ashamed of himself."

Roberts's wife, however, insisted, "The man that did this . . . was not the Charley I've been married to for almost ten years. My husband was loving, supportive, thoughtful.

Two Amish girls on their way to school.

All the things you'd always want and more. He was an exceptional father [who] took the kids to soccer practice and games, played ball in the backyard and took our seven-year-old daughter shopping. He never said no when I asked him to change a diaper." Other family members who had seen Roberts the night before the murders said they never suspected anything was wrong with him.

FORGIVENESS

Across the Internet, bloggers described Roberts as "sick," "evil," "disgusting"—but the people he had hurt the most, the Amish community, reached out with immediate compassion and forgiveness to Roberts's wife and family. On the day of the shooting, a grandfather of one of the murdered Amish girls reminded younger members of the community, "We must not think evil of this man." Another Amish father said, "He had a mother and a wife and a soul and now he's standing before a just God." One of the fathers of the dead girls said, "The pain of the killer's parents is ten times my pain. You would just feel terrible if you were the parent of a killer."

Jack Meyer, a member of another religious community living near the Amish in Lancaster County, explained: "I don't think there's anybody here that wants to do anything but forgive and not only reach out to those who have suffered a loss in that way but to reach out to the family of the man who committed these acts."

The Roberts family was amazed and grateful when Amish community members visited and comforted them. The Amish normally do not mix with others from outside their community, but in this time of terrible tragedy, they reached out past their boundaries. The father of a slain daughter explained, "our forgiveness was not our words, it was what we did." For nearly an hour, one Amish man held Roberts's sobbing father in his arms, comforting him. They hugged Roberts's widow and other members of his family; they brought food and flowers to the Roberts's home. Of the seventy-five people at the killer's burial, over half were Amish, including parents who had buried their own children a day or so before. The Amish community also set up a charitable fund for Roberts's family.

Marie Roberts, the shooter's wife, wrote an open letter to her Amish neighbors, thanking them for their forgiveness:

> Your love for our family has helped to provide the healing we so desperately need. Gifts you've given have touched our hearts in a way no words can describe. Your compassion has reached beyond our family, beyond our community, and is changing our world, and for this we sincerely thank you.

Some news commentators criticized the Amish community's attitude of such immediate and total forgiveness. Across North America, many people felt the community's forgiveness made no sense; it even seemed inappropriate. Terrible evil had been done; how could the Amish not react with normal, healthy anger?

Donald Craybill and other scholars of Amish life noted that "letting go of grudges" is a deeply-rooted value in Amish culture; they explained that the Amish willingness to forgo vengeance does not undo the tragedy or pardon the wrong, "If Roberts had lived, we would have forgiven him, but there would have been consequences," explained an Amish minister. Regardless of violence's necessary consequences, however, for the Amish, forgiveness is the first step toward a future that is more hopeful.

The Amish are simple people who have thought deeply about some of life's most difficult issues.

NEW HOPE

As a symbol of their attitude toward the violence that had invaded their community, the week after the shooting, the Amish at Nickel Mines tore down the building where it had happened. A new schoolhouse, called the New Hope School, was built at a differ-

Why Do the Amish Believe in Forgiveness?

According to a *Philadelphia Inquirer* op ed piece by Donald Kraybill, an expert in Amish life, the earliest founders of the Amish culture, the Anabaptist martyrs, "emphasized yielding one's life completely to God." He went on to say:

Songs by imprisoned Anabaptists, recorded in the *Ausbund*, the Amish hymn book, are regularly used in Amish church services today. The 1,200-page *Martyrs Mirror*, first printed in 1660, which tells the martyr stories, is found in many Amish houses and is cited by preachers in their sermons. The martyr voice still rings loudly in Amish ears with the message of forgiveness of those who tortured them and burned their bodies at the stake.

The martyr testimony springs from the example of Jesus, the cornerstone of Amish faith. As do other Anabaptists, the Amish take the life and teachings of Jesus seriously. . . . Retaliation and revenge are not part of their vocabulary.

ent location, near the original site; it opened on April 2, 2007, exactly six months after the shooting. The new school was intentionally built as "different" as possible from the original, including the style of the flooring.

Clearly, the members of the Nickel Mines community had been deeply shaken by what had happened. They wholeheartedly rejected the violence that had taken their children. As they sorrowed for their children, they struggled to put their lives back together—but before they even began their own mourning, they forgave the killer who had brought them such sorrow.

A father who lost a daughter in the schoolhouse told author Donald Kraybill, "Forgiveness means giving up the right to revenge." Another Amish man explained that "the acid of bitterness eats the container that holds it." This doesn't mean that the Amish don't believe that the **perpetrators** of violence shouldn't face consequences; if Roberts had not killed himself, the Amish would have

perpetrators: those who commit a crime or wrongdoing.

The Amish hymnal shown here was written in the seventeenth century. It includes stories of martyrs who gave their lives for their faith.

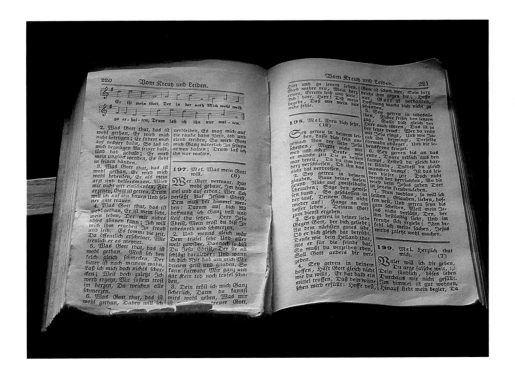

believed he should have been arrested and imprisoned—but in order to protect others from his violence, rather than out of revenge. According to Kraybill, the "Amish believe that God smiles on acts of grace that open doors for reconciliation." In *Amish Grace: How Forgiveness Transcended Tragedy*, Kraybill, with coauthors Steven Nolt and David Weaver-Zercher, wrote:

> For the Amish, . . . the preferred way to live on with meaning and hope is to offer forgiveness—and offer it quickly. That offer, including the willingness to forgo vengeance, does not undo the tragedy or pardon the wrong. It does, however, constitute a first step toward a future

that is more hopeful, and potentially less violent, than it would otherwise be.

SCHOOL VIOLENCE— WHAT'S THE ANSWER?

The shooting at Nickel Mines schoolhouse shook the United States—especially since it was the third school shooting in less than a week. Earlier that week, on September 27, a gunman had killed a student and then shot himself at Platte Canyon High School in Bailey, Colorado; two days later, at Weston High School in Wisconsin, a student had shot and

This map shows the enormous scope of school violence across the United States.

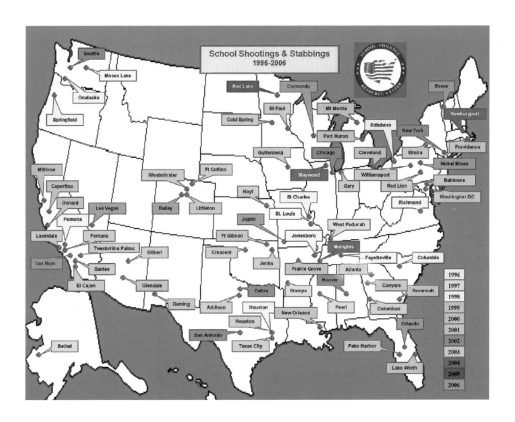

killed the principal. Nickel Mines was the twenty-fourth school shooting in the United States in 2006.

The Bush administration held a conference to discuss the issue of school violence. School districts across the country—and around the world—tried to understand the problem. New programs were implemented, new regulations were passed, and communities worked together to try to find the answers to a complicated and terrifying problem.

While government and school officials work to make schools safer, the Amish community's response continues to challenge the world to consider a new approach to violence. In a world where our safety is threatened (whether by school shootings or terrorists), it would be all too easy to respond with fear and hatred. Psychologists, however, agree that the Amish community's attitude of forgiveness is far more healthy, both for themselves and for the entire world.

THE BENEFITS OF FORGIVENESS

Humans often find it hard to forgive when they've been injured—but doctors and psychologists have found that forgiveness, no matter how difficult, is good for us, both emotionally and physically. The subject is one of the hottest fields of research in clinical psychology today, with more than 1,200 published studies, up from just 58 as recently as 1997. Forgiveness research even has its own foundation: A Campaign for Forgiveness Research.

Studies suggest that forgiveness reduces stress. In the process, blood pressure drops and **hormonal** changes occur, both of which have been linked to **cardiovascular** disease, **immune suppression** and, possibly **impaired neurological** function and memory. "It happens down the line, but every time you feel unforgiveness, you are more likely to develop a health problem," says Everett Worthington, executive director of A Campaign for Forgiveness Research.

People who can forgive are also able to build closer relationships with others (as the Amish have), while those who nurse their grudges tend to isolate themselves. Research shows that people with strong social networks tend to be healthier than loners. Forgiveness, says Charlotte van Oyen Witvliet, a researcher at Hope College in Holland, Michigan, should be a way of life, not merely a response to specific insults.

Archbishop Tutu, who survived years of racial violence in South Africa, is another firm believer in the power of forgiveness to transform both individuals and the world.

hormonal: related to or affected by hormones, substances produced by the body to bring about physiological changes.

cardiovascular: relating to the heart and blood vessels.

immune suppression: keeping the immune system, which helps the body fight off infections, from working properly or efficiently.

impaired: weakened, damaged, not functioning correctly.

neurological: relating to the nerves.

The Amish, shown here tending their graves, have a hopeful perspective on death.

Tutu, who received a Nobel Peace Prize for his efforts to reconcile blacks and whites in Sout Africa, writes:

> When I talk of forgiveness I mean the belief that you can come out the other side a better person. A better person than the one being consumed by anger and hatred. Remaining in that state locks you in a state of victimhood, making you almost dependent on the perpetrator. If you can find it in yourself to forgive then you are no longer chained to the perpetrator. You can move on, and you can even help the perpetrator to become a better person too.

The authors of *Amish Grace* acknowledge, "In a culture that places such a premium on buying and selling, as opposed to giving and receiving, forgiveness runs against the grain." They go on to say:

> Running against that grain, finding alternative ways to imagine our world, ways that in turn will facilitate forgiveness, takes more than individual willpower. We are not only the products of our culture, we are also producers of our culture. We need to construct cultures that value and nurture forgiveness. In their own way, the Amish have constructed such an environment. The challenge for the rest of us is to use

our resources creatively to shape cultures that discourage revenge as a first response. How might we work more imaginatively to create communities in which enemies are treated as members of the human family and not demonized? How might these communities foster visions that enable their members to see offenders, as well as victims, as persons with authentic needs? There are no simple answers to these questions, though any answer surely will involve the habits we decide to value, the images we choose to celebrate, and the stories we remember. . . .

In a world where faith often justifies and magnifies revenge, and in a nation

The New Hope Schoolhouse was built to replace the old one that was a scene of such terrible violence.

According to Dr. Fred Luskin, author of *Forgive for Good: A Proven Prescription for Health and Happiness*:

Forgiveness is NOT . . .

- condoning violence or unkindness.

- forgetting that something painful happened.

- excusing violence or unkind behaviors.

- a necessarily religious or spiritual experience.

- reconciling with the offender.

- denying your own feelings of pain.

- a way to change or evade the past.

- canceling out the consequences or legal compensation for violence.

- lying down and being a doormat for people to walk on.

where some Christians use scripture to fuel retaliation, the Amish response was indeed a surprise. Regardless of the details of the Nickel Mines story, one message rings clear: religion was used not to justify rage and revenge but to inspire goodness, forgiveness, and grace. And that is the big lesson for the rest of us regardless of our faith or nationality.

Violence creates vicious circles. The kids who are bullied sometimes turn around and become killers. This tends to make students less accepting of other kids who are different . . . and the cycle continues.

As the Amish stress, violence once committed must be dealt with; we need laws and consequences to protect us. Meanwhile, however, practicing forgiveness might help us build a world where violence no longer seemed like the answer to people who were frustrated and angry. It might actually make our schools and communities safer places to live.

Further Reading

De Lint, Charles. *The Blue Girl*. New York, N.Y.: Puffin, 2006.

Kraybill, Donald B., Steven M. Nolt, and David L. Weaver. *Amish Grace: How Forgiveness Transcended Tragedy*. San Francisco, Calif.: Jossey-Bass, 2007.

Langman, Peter. *Why Kids Kill: Inside the Minds of School Shooters*. New York, N.Y.: Palgrave Macmillan, 2009.

Lindholm, Marjorie. *A Columbine Survivor's Story*. Littleton, Col.: Regenold Publishing, 2005.

Merritt, Rob. *No Easy Answers: The Truth Behind Death at Columbine*. New York, N.Y.: Lantern Books, 2002.

Meyer, Adam. *The Last Domino*. New York, N.Y.: Putnam, 2005.

Sprague, Susan. *Coping with Cliques: A Workbook to Help Girls Deal with Gossip, Put-Downs, Bullying, & Other Mean Behavior*. New York, N.Y.: New Harbinger, 2008.

For More Information

Amish Grace
www.amishgrace.com

The Columbine Report
www.cnn.com/SPECIALS/2000/columbine.
   cd/frameset.exclude.htm

Stories of Surviving Bullying
www.geocities.com/gold_blood_uk/
   Bullyingstories.html

Surviving Bullies Project
survivingbullies.com

Ten Myths About School Shootings
www.msnbc.msn.com/id/15111438

Virginia Tech: We Remember
www.vt.edu/remember

Publisher's note:
The Web sites listed on this page were active at the time of publication. The publisher is not responsible for Web sites that have changed their addresses or discontinued operation since the date of publication. The publisher will review and update the Web-site list upon each reprint.

Bibliography

Biography of William J. Clinton. www.white-house.gov/history/presidents/bc42.htm.

Carlson, E. B. and Dalenberg, C. J. "A Conceptual Framework for the Impact of Traumatic Experiences." *Trauma, Violence, & Abuse*, pp. 1, 4–28, 2000.

Celebrity Anecdotes. www.anecdote.com.

Chris Rock. www.chrisrock.com.

Christina Aguilera. wwwchristinaaguilera.com.

Clinton Foundation. www.clintonfoundation.org.

Cloke, Kenneth. *Mediating Dangerously: The Frontiers of Conflict Resolution*. San Francisco, Calif.: Jossey-Bass, 2001.

Cose, Ellis. B*one To Pick: Of Forgiveness, Reconciliation, Reparation, and Revenge*. New York, N.Y.: Atria Books, 2004.

Enright, Robert D. and Richard P. Fitzgibbons. *Helping Clients Forgive: An Empirical Guide for Resolving Anger and Restoring Hope*. Washington, D.C.: American Psychological Association, 2000.

Goode, E. "Therapists Hear Survivors' Refrain: 'If Only.'" *New York Times, Science Times*, p. 1, November 25, 2001.

Bibliography

Govier, Trudy. *Forgiveness and Revenge*. New York, N.Y.: Routledge, 2002.

Harrison Ford. www.harrison-ford.com/bio.htm.

KidsHealth. "School Violence and the News." kidshealth.org/parent/positive/talk/school_violence.html.

Lifton, R. J. "From Hiroshima to Nazi Doctors: The Evolution of Psychoformative Approaches to Understanding Traumatic Stress Syndromes, pp. 11–23. In J. P. Wilson & B. Raphael (eds). *International Handbook of Traumatic Stress Syndromes*. New York, N.Y.: Plenum Press, 1993.

Luskin, Fred. *Forgive for Good: A Proven Prescription for Health and Happiness*. San Francisco, Calif.: HarperCollins, 2002.

Nader, Kathleen. Gift from Within—PTSD Resources for Survivors and Caregivers. www.giftfromwithin.org/html/guilt.html.

Prager, Carol A.L., and Trudy Govier, eds. *Dilemmas of Reconciliation*. Waterloo, Ont.: Wilfrid Laurier University Press, 2003.

Schiraldi, G. R. *The Post-Traumatic Stress Disorder Source Book*. Los Angeles, Calif.: Lowell House, 2000.

Bibliography

Shriver, Donald W. Jr. "Forgiveness: A Bridge Across Abysses of Revenge." In *Forgiveness and Reconciliation*, edited by Raymond Helmick and Rodney Petersen, 151–170. New York, N.Y.: Templeton Foundation Press, 2001.

TeenTouch. "Facts of Bullying." www.teen-touch.org/coping_bullies.asp.

Tiger Woods, wwwtigerwoods.com.

Tutu, Desmond. *No Future Without Forgiveness*. New York, N.Y.: Doubleday, 1999.

World Health Organization. "Bullying and Symptoms Among School-Aged Children: International Comparative Cross Sectional Study in 28 Countries." *European Journal of Public Health*, Vol. 15, No. 2, pp. 128–132, 2005.

Worthington, Everett L. *Five Steps to Forgiveness: The Art and Science of Forgiving*. New York, N.Y.: Crown Publishers, 2001.

Index

Index

Picture Credits

cc-a 2.0: p. 71, 76, 114-115
  Chesi-Fotos CC: p. 82, 86
  de Castro, Elysson: p. 77
  Eddie-s: p. 85
  Fernandez, Steven: p. 61
  flyagain: p. 23, 31
  indio: p. 75
  Phelps, James: p. 70

cc-a-sa 3.0
  Qqqqqq: p. 20

cc-a-sa 2.0: p. 44-45
  timsnell: p. 74
  watchwithkristin: p. 78

Columbine High School Yearbook: p. 29

Dreamstime Images
  Burkhard, Sascha: p. 17
  Gadjoboy: p. 94
  Godfer: p. 54, 81
  Gunion, Richard: p. 99
  Iushewitz, David: p. 8
  Jensen, Derek: p. 96–97
  Littel, Marco: p. 109
  Mettendorf, Ernest: p. 107

MW Productions: p. 57
Opris, Constantin: p. 11
Strathdee, Stephen: p. 15
York, Chris: p. 103

Federal Bureau of Investigation: p 25

GNU Free Documentation License 1.2
  Damiano, William Chase: p. 36
  UserB: p. 34, 48

Hufschmid, Eric: p. 22

Istockphotos.com
  Coffey, Mark: p. 90
  Driscoll, Christopher O.: p. 88

Jupiter Images: p. 52

PR Photos
  Mayer, Janet: p. 46, 48

United States Geological Survey: p. 24

www.whitehouse.gov: p. 16, 43, 46, 51, 72, 73, 79

To the best knowledge of the publisher, all images not specifically credited are in the public domain. If any image has been inadvertently uncredited, please notify Harding House Publishing Service, 220 Front Street, Vestal, New York 13850, so that credit can be given in future printings.

About the Author and the Consultant

Author

Rae Simons has written many books for young adults. She lives in New York State, and is the mother of three teenage children. With a background in psychology and education, Rae has worked in middle schools and high schools, and she has observed firsthand both sides of the bullying equation.

Consultant

Andrew M. Kleiman, M.D. is a Clinical Instructor in Psychiatry at New York University School of Medicine. He received a BA in philosophy from the University of Michigan, and graduated from Tulane University School of Medicine. Dr. Kleiman completed his internship, residency, and fellowship in psychiatry at New York University and Bellevue Hospital. He is currently in private practice in Manhattan and teaches at New York University School of Medicine.